YOUR KNOWLEDGE HAS VALUE

- We will publish your bachelor's and master's thesis, essays and papers

- Your own eBook and book - sold worldwide in all relevant shops

- Earn money with each sale

Upload your text at www.GRIN.com
and publish for free

Bibliographic information published by the German National Library:

The German National Library lists this publication in the National Bibliography; detailed bibliographic data are available on the Internet at http://dnb.dnb.de .

Imprint:

Copyright © 2017 GRIN Verlag
Print and binding: Books on Demand GmbH, Norderstedt Germany
ISBN: 9783668714540

Rohan Ahmed

SAPUI5 and Fiori. Status and Future Perspective

GRIN Verlag

GRIN - Your knowledge has value

Since its foundation in 1998, GRIN has specialized in publishing academic texts by students, college teachers and other academics as e-book and printed book. The website www.grin.com is an ideal platform for presenting term papers, final papers, scientific essays, dissertations and specialist books.

Visit us on the internet:

SAPUI5 and Fiori - Status and Future Perspective

Rohan Ahmed

[1] Heilbronn University, Course Business Informatics,

19.01.2017 – version 1

Abstract

Today almost every software and websites has a mobile compatible version and everyone can check anything on his mobile or tablet. This wasn't the case 7-8 years ago. For SAP, Graphical User Interface as known as GUI was very powerful at the time when SAP launched its ERP software. With time, many other software exists with the fleet of HTML5 based powerful and more appealing modern UI-technology. For this, the old GUI was not able to stand with it. As everyone knows, today are smartphones and tablets more powerful than pc's. So, it was very important for SAP to find a solution and its was SAP Fiori – "One UX for all SAP Products". Fiori is based on a framework known as SAPUI5 which is built on top of HTML5 and is compatible with any device and any screen size. The first announcement from SAP about Fiori was in May 2013 with the first release of 25 transactional Fiori apps for the most common business functions, such as self-services tasks which known as ESS/MSS. Today, there are more than 1140 true Fiori apps available in Fiori library. The number of apps can partially supplement the previous GUI transactions. SAP offers three types of Fiori apps with different database requirements. A distinction is made between Transactional apps, Analytical apps and factsheets. Only Transactional apps can run on any database that supports SAP ERP. The other 2 types require SAP HANA as database. Since 2013, Fiori has made great progress and will continue in the coming years.

1 Introduction

In this seminar thesis, you will get a view on SAP UI5 and Fiori – Status and future perspective. So, what is SAP? SAP was founded in 1972 in Walldorf, Germany. The acronym SAP stands for "Systems, Applications and Products in Data Processing" [10]. Over the years SAP become the world premier provider of client/server business solutions [10]. Today, SAP has a good reputation worldwide. Fiori is the most important technology for modern SAP user interfaces in the coming years. It offers more than nice surface elements, such as cross-application functions as well as a sophisticated design process. With this, Fiori apps lead more efficiency for users in the operation of SAP applications. Fiori presents the user with SAP applications in the form of apps. There are already several hundred standard SAP applications, such as Finance, Logistics and CRM. SAP customers and service providers can also develop their own Fiori Apps [13]. Fiori Apps are web applications that can be run not only on any desktop PC, nut also on all current tablets and smartphones and in any browser. This means, that the use of this application also be possible without the mouse and keyboard, with fingers and screen keyboard. Depending on the format of the used display, the user interface is automatically adapted through Responsive Design [13].

1.1 Problem Statement

SAP GUI is a fundamental problem that SAP has been struggling for a long time. GUI is a graphical user interface that was released in the basic functionality more than 15 years ago. SAP has recognized that programs and users' needs have changed since the proliferation of smartphones and apps. By a simple and intuitive operation, a better user experience can be provided. Fiori is a new SAP UI-Technology with modern design for a rediscovered user experience. SAP Fiori delivers a role-based, consumer-grade user experience across all lines of business, tasks, and devices.

1.2 Goal

The main goal of this study is to analyze the literature in reference to SAP UI5 and Fiori and get information about the status in the present time and the future perspective of this SAP technology.

1.3. Structure of seminar thesis

First, an overview into the various terminology will be given, which are relevant for this topic. In the next chapter, the researched methodology is introducing. After that, a comparison between Fiori in the present and Fiori in the future is shown. Then the SAP Fiori UX Design Principles are briefly introduced and to the connection the three SAP Fiori types are explained. Lastly, the differences between Fiori and WebDynpro ABAP are shown in a table. To get an insight into the subject, the literature "Beginning SAP Fiori" from the author Mathew, B. was used [3].

2   Fundamentals and basic Terms

2.1   SAP GUI

SAP GUI is an acronym and is standing for SAP Graphical User Interface. A SAP User uses this GUI as a frontend. The SAP GUI is similar in functionality to a web browser but more specialized in the presentation of content in the SAP type "Look and Feel". In contrast to a standard browser, the SAP GUI manages session relevant data on the client, which minimizes the communication requirements on the server. The advantage of this is that the SAP applications can react quickly to user input. In this way, the SAP GUI provides a uniform access point to all SAP functions and is still lean. In addition, it allows to extend the given system by programming [1]. Zairi et. al. describes the main three responsibilities of SAP GUI like: "(1) presenting all data to the end-users; (2) creating all GUI components, such as window and buttons, and taking on all user inputs; and (3) communicating all user requests and inputs to SAP applications across the network" [2].

2.2   SAP Fiori

When SAP launched the ERP software, the GUI for SAP was a powerful piece at that time. But today we all know the power of smartphones, ultrabooks and tablets and this is the reason why the old desktop based SAP GUI is getting outdated. SAP's solution to their ageing GUI is today SAP Fiori. Fiori is a based on a framework known UI5 (see below 2.2 and 2.3), which is built on top of HTML5. Fiori offers, like many other software products on the market, to be compatible with any device with any screen size. Fiori is the highlight from SAP to achieve their new goal of "One UX for all SAP Products" [3]. Fiori provides increased user productivity by simplifying and automating tasks on any device, increased user acceptance through an appealing user experience design on the most important tasks and activities. It also provides improved compliance and data quality by easily capturing enterprise data. As well reduce training and support costs through simple, roll-based screens that reduce training time and minimize user errors, but also a simple extension or programming of customer-specific SAP Fiori apps with technologies and development tools from SAP.

2.3   SAPUI5

SAPUI5 is the next generation of Web Dynpro ABAP (show below: 2.5.) and the latest SAP interface technology. SAPUI5 is a client UI technology based on JavaScript, CSS and HTML5. Fiori apps developed with SAPUI5 framework can run in a browser on any device. As in the past, no SAP GUI is necessary to develop a UI5 application. It is enough when Eclipse is installed as a development environment. The UI5 applications can communicate with the SAP backend via HTTP (Hypertext Transfer Protocol) requests via the ICM (Internet Communication Manager). It is possible to create your own services to exchange data with the backend, or use the SAP NetWeaver Gateway.

2.4   Open UI5

OpenUI5 is an Open Source JavaScript UI library, maintained by SAP and available under the Apache 2.0 license while SAPUI5 is the version that may be used by SAP Customer with a certain kind of license [5]. The usage of SAPUI5 is also free for customers, but they pay for other SAP products. However the most of the features of both UI5 technologies are identical.

2.5 Web Dynpro ABAP

"Web Dynpro ABAP is part of the presentation layer and it's the SAP standard UI technology used for developing web business application without knowing HTML or JavaScript" [4]. To understand: The biggest difference between WebDynpro ABAP and Fiori apps are - a WebDynpro application cannot run on any smartphones or tablet instead only on a browser enabled laptop or desktop pc.

3 Methodology for the literature work

3.1 Literature references

The following literature databases are used to determine the analysis the literature.

#	Name of Database's	Acronym
L1	Google Scholar	GS
L2	SAP Press	SAP Press
L3	ScienceDirect[1]	SD
L4	Springer Link	SL
L5	GBI-Genios Deutsche Wirtschaftsdatenbank	WISO

Table 1: Used Databases for the seminar thesis

3.2 Filters

SAPUI5 and Fiori was announced from SAP in 2013, so there was no need to set a filter for literature research. Only English and German literature were used.

3.3 Search terms

To find literatures in relation to SAPUI5 and Fiori, following search terms are used:

- SAPUI5
- Fiori
- SAP User experience
- Web Dynpro ABAP
- SAP UI-technology

3.4 Result for the literature search

In the search, could be established that there are many literatures for SAPUI5 and Fiori, but this covered mostly the technical part, which is not include in this seminar thesis. Another point, which was noticed is, that there are more books from SAP instead of papers or other kind of literatures. And these books are only available for a fee. Therefore, more online references were used for this seminar.

---

[1] http://www.sciencedirect.com/

4

4   Results

4.1   Fiori apps in the present and in the future

The first announcement from SAP about Fiori was in May 2013 which includes 25 Fiori apps for the most common business functions, such as workflow approvals, information lookup and self-services tasks which known as ESS/MSS [9]. SAP said, that this way allows the business users to perform their daily tasks by creating a more intuitive format and user experience and compares this technique with the technology in everyday life [9].

A quote appears in SAP News from Vishal Sikka, who is a member of the Executive Board of SAP AG, Technology and Innovation: "We are on a mission to renew the experience across all of our applications. Users demand simplicity and ease of use, and SAP Fiori brings this experience to our customers. SAP customers can adopt SAP Fiori immediately and bring instant value to all their employees" [9].

At the time of research, December 2016, there are the Fiori library hold around 1140 true Apps in SAP Fiori library. The number of apps (1140) can partially supplement the previous GUI transactions.

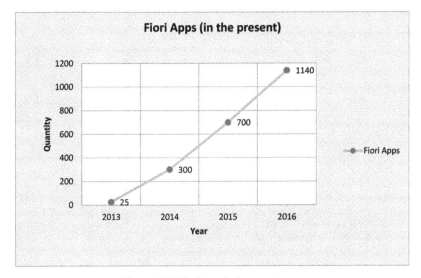

Figure 1: SAP Fiori Apps in the present

The line chart (figure 1) shows the permanent growing number of Fiori apps since 2013. In May 2013 was the first release of 25 Fiori apps. Now there are about 1140 Fiori apps available [8]. With a simple calculation, there is an average of about 30 apps per month or you can say about 360 apps per year but the number of developed apps can however increase.

The interesting question that arises from this is, when will it happen, that all SAP GUI transaction liked to HANA will be developed and the use of SAP GUI is no longer needed?

There are about 6500 classic GUI transactions liked to HANA implementations [8]. So, we can compare the existed number of Fiori apps (1140) and the number of classic GUI transactions (about 6500) and see how many works be remaining in the backlog of SAP [8]. With the use of simple calculation above, it will give us a projection of more than 20 years to complete the work in their backlog, see in figure 2 below.

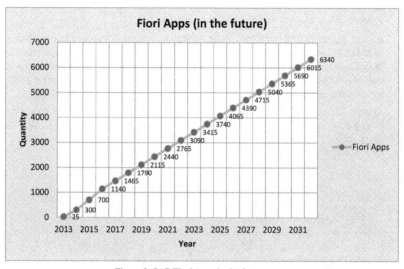

Figure 2: SAP Fiori Apps in the future

But it is also to noticed, that the relationship between SAP GUI transactions and Fiori apps is not one-to-one. It is possible, that in one SAP GUI transaction may be multiple Fiori apps include, or multiple SAP GUI transaction into a single Fiori app [8]. For example, the self-service scenario offers to kind of leave requests for employee. One kind is absence request and the second one is holiday request. This can be done, for example in a single Fiori app. If we take this into consideration, the above shown figure 1 will no longer be correct and could be possible for SAP to replaces the old GUI much earlier. To this end, SAP published in his SAP News: "The SAP Fiori apps can be deployed in multiple ways; as a collection of apps with a single Launchpad, as multiple Web apps, and they can be consumed from SAP or third-party" [9].

4.2 SAP Fiori UX Design Principles

With the use of SAP Fiori UX Design Principles is meant, that employees can expect a consumer-grade user experience [11]. "Enterprise apps now demand to be more intuitive, personalized, and thoroughly designed in the way they are utilized" [11]. SAP now offers these requirements with Fiori Apps.

- Improve productivity by ensuring simplicity and automated task completion [11].
- Easy development of Fiori applications using SAP development tools and technology [11]
- Cost reduction for training and support by simple, roll-screened screens [11]
- Enhances user adoption through UX design [11]
- Enhances data quality and compliance guaranteeing ease in system record entry [11]

SAP Fiori UX Design Principles

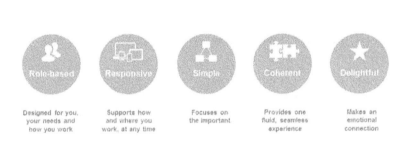

Figure 3: SAP Fiori UX Design Principles[2]

SAP Fiori brings great user experience to enterprise applications [12]. "Based on user roles and business processes, SAP Fiori simplifies doing business" [12].

The five UX Design Principles of SAP Fiori design are briefly introduced below:

Role-based

SAP describes the role-based principle as "Designed for you, your needs and how you work". Each Fiori app is specific to a user's role. These can, for example a manager, an employee or a salesperson. But as you know it from everyday life, a user can have multiple roles. So, it is possible to assigned a user to different modules like HR, CRM, SRM and so on [3].

Responsive

This principle "Supports how and where you work, at any time". It is possible to run Fiori app on any browser and any device, because it's HTML5-based. Also, Fiori supports multiple interaction modes, such as keyboards, touch gesture and mice. The best about Fiori Apps is, that there are works independently of all kind of platforms [3].

---

[2] https://experience.sap.com/news/asug-webcast-recap-sap-fiori-deep-dive/

Simple

Fiori Apps are simple and focused on the important part. So, that helps user to complete their tasks quickly and easily. Compared to old GUI transactions, it is a big change. "Fiori apps emphasize a 1:1:3 approach: one user, one use case, and three screens (desktop, tablet, and mobile)" [3].

Coherent

In short "Provides one fluid, seamless experience". It does not matter how many Fiori Apps SAP offers. They all have the same design footprint and thus the same look and feel [3]. This makes the handling easier for the user and the user feel comfortable with other Fiori apps after using one.

Delightful

The motto under this principle is "Makes an emotional connection". It makes your workplace job role easier and smarter. And this also save costs. The UI is simple to understand and follows the same design pattern across apps.

4.3 SAP Fiori App Types

It is interesting to know that SAP offers three types of Fiori apps with different database requirements. These apps distinguished by their focus and infrastructure requirements. A distinction is made between:

o   Transactional apps

o   Analytical apps

o   Fact sheets

The SAP Fiori Apps can be accessed via the Intranet (inside the company network). It is also possible to access the apps over the Internet (outside the company network), but ensuring data security is a prerequisite. To understand the different between the three SAP Fiori apps, a short explanation is given:

4.3.1 Transactional apps

As one can imagine, transactional apps are used to perform transactional tasks for example creating a leave request for an employee. The optimal basis for this app type is HANA, but it is also possible to use any other type of database that SAP ERP supports with sufficient performance. Figure 4 below give an overview how transactional Fiori apps are deployed and consumed by the end users [3]:

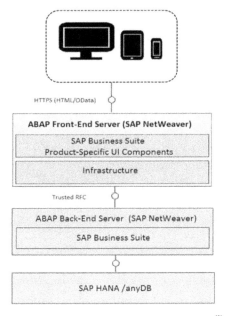

Figure 4:   **Fiori transactional app architecture** [3]

The first block shows the devices. It can be a desktop, tablets or mobile devices, that access the Fiori Launchpad. The second block show the ABAP frontend server contained the UI layer, which has product specific UI components for the Fiori apps, for example UI-add-ons can be for ERP specific tasks. The infrastructure block contains the SAPUI5 libraries, Fiori Launchpad components and SAP Gateway. The components communicate with the next block ABAP back-end server trough RFC (requests for comments). In the last block is the database stored. Transactional Fiori apps can run on HANA database or any other database supported by SAP R/3[3].

4.3.2   Analytical apps

"Analytical applications give users access to real-time data regarding the business. These apps collect and process a huge amount of data in a matter of seconds and present the results in a simplified format that the user can understand and relate to easily." [3]

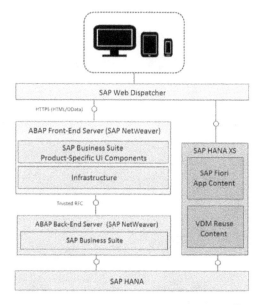

Figure 5:   **Fiori analytical app architecture** [3]

The ABAP front-end server is like transactional apps, which contains the UI layer. The infrastructure layer contains the SAP UI libraries, Fiori Launchpad and SAP Gateway with the OData service enabled [3]. The frontend-server use trusted RFC to communicate with the ABAP backend-server, which contains the business logic. The block on the right is SAP HANA XS, which is also contains Fiori app content for the relevant business suite products, framework for KPI modeling, a generic drill-down app and the virtual data model [3]. Analytical apps can run only on SAP HANA with use of virtual data models structured representations of SAP HANA database views [3]. "VDMs provide direct access to SAP business data by using standard SQL or OData requests" [3]. The Web Dispatcher on the top identifies the incoming requests targets and reroutes the requests accordingly [3].

4.3.3 Fact sheets

Fact sheets show contextual information and the most important aspects of central objects used in business processes. These apps allow you to use the drill down option to display detailed information, or navigate from a fact sheet to the associated fact sheets. For example, it is possible to access backend system from a fact sheet for a document to display the details or to edit the document in SAP GUI or Web-Dynpro Application. The displayed data is retrieved from the SAP HANA database, mainly using search engines.

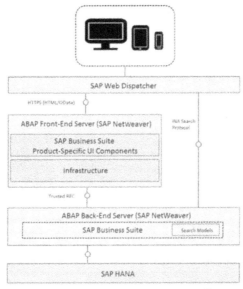

Figure 6:   Fiori fact sheet architecture [3]

Same as analytical apps, fact sheet apps run only on SAP HANA. The ABAP frontend server is the same as for transactional and analytical apps. Users can start transactions by navigating into transactional apps, access backend systems and so on. „The frontend server reads the access to the ABAP backend server via trusted RFC connections. The backend server contains the business suite with relevant business logic, OData services for the apps, and search models [3]."

4.4   Difference between SAPUI5 and Web-Dynpro ABAP

SAP UI5 framework is getting increasingly important for SAP web application developers. Also, SAP has big plans on Fiori, to use mobile web applications on SAP, built on SAPUI5 & SAP Gateway. It is a big step for SAP to move from WebDynpro to UI5 development. The table below shows the key differences between these two commonly used UI frameworks from SAP.

Feature	Web-Dynpro ABAP	SAPUI5 & OpenUI5
UI technology	• Limited UI features • Limited customization possible	• Latest web UI features available • Ability to customize and extend
Browser	• Applications run on the server side • On laptop or desktop pc	• Run in any browser on any device

Scenarios	• Build desktop based applications • Simple and complex screens	• "Code Once - Run on Any Device" [6] • Simple screens
Development skills	• ABAP	• HTML/HTML5 & CSS • JavaScript/JQuery
Platforms & Tools	• SAP ABAP stack – for WebDynpro • NWDS & NWDI	• SAP ABAP stack • SAP HANA XS • Eclipse with UI5 plugins • (Tomcat)
Mobile support	• Not supported	• Fully supported with dedicated mobile libraries for UI
Models	• Java, ABAP, Web services models	• OData & JSON

Table 2: Difference between WebDynpro ABAP and SAPUI5

Now it is clear that SAP UI5 is based on the most modern web development standards of today, namely on HMTL5, CSS and JavaScript. With this, SAP plans to offer state-of-the-art and platform-independent applications, which can also run on mobile devices. The applications run directly in the browser, regardless of the operating system, be it Android or iOS. The disadvantage is, that the apps are not offline available, but all popular browsers are supported [7].

In the Eclipse IDE, the UI5 applications can be created. These are developed just like Web Dynpro case per the model view controller architecture. Various data models like JSON, XML, Resource and OData Model are available [7].

4.5 Fiori compared to WebDynpro Application

In this chapter, we are going to compare a Web Dynpro Application with the new Fiori Application. It will also be interesting to see how the old WDA design differs from the new Fiori design. Are there many differences?

In the following two figures showed below, the self-service scenario "Leave Request" are compared. But first the similarities between Fiori and WebDynpro Application are illustrated:

- All services are free. Only ESS/MSS license is required
- Both types of application have the same basic customizing
- Both have same request database and
- same workflow logic for approval processes

Figure 7: WebDynpro ABAP – Leave request

Figure 7 shows a screenshot of the self-service scenario leave request developed in standard WebDynpro for ABAP. The main advantage of the standard WebDynpro application was the reduction of the administrative costs in the human resources by employee services. In the above UI building block, you can see a calendar for the next three months. The legend (absent, transmitted, day off and so on) is displayed in color below the calendar. In the lower UI building block shows the details. You can add here one or more approvers. It is also possible to select the type of leave.

According to mindsquare [14] this WebDynpro application is linked to HR Releases and offers the following pros and cons:

Pros:

- Comprehensive illustration of service
- Good and easy customization of the service based on known technologies
- Proven and stable applications

Cons:

- WebDynpro applications are not suitable for mobile use
- Low user acceptance

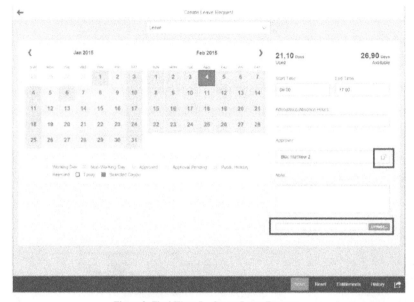

Figure 8: Fiori Wave 7 – Create Leave Request

The first impression is good! The highlight of SAP – Fiori apps. Similarities with Figure 7 can be seen. The differences are, that you see the calendar of the next two months and the details are not in the lower UI building block, but on the right site, which offers the user an advantage of the clarity. In the header area, you can select the type of leave. In the top of right you can see the used and available leaves. The send button is on the button, as we know it in everyday life and not in the top like WebDynpro application. The scope of functions is restricted here; you can't select more than one approver, which was possible in WebDynpro application (see figure 7). But contrary to WDA, the handling of the app looks easier.

Mindsquare [14] also presents for Fiori the following pros and cons:

Pros:

- Fiori apps are not linked to HR Releases and can be installed as a separated component

- You can run Fiori apps on any mobile according to the new SAP User Experience strategy

- Technology is future-oriented and very simple to understand for users.

- Customizable to customer needs

Cons:

- Reduced functionality and so far, a few services are available.

- Existing adjustments in WebDynpro applications will not be considered.

14

5   Conclusion

It will be very exciting how the approach of SAP Fiori Apps in the wide market can be implemented and how SAP replace the old GUI with Fiori. The publication of SAP also helps to make the user interface Fiori a free component of SAP software. The mobile surfaces in a Fiori apps were at the launch delicately, but now they are acceptable. The separation between the user interface and the backend is also a logical step by SAP. This allows SAP to react quickly to upcoming challenges. In combination with the use of common standards, like HTML5, CSS, JQuery and OData, a technological flexibility for the future is gained. But also, the approach of the device independence, which SAP has taken, is correct. This is the only way to react to the fast-moving market. SAPUI5 frameworks which is needed to develop Fiori apps is becoming increasingly important for SAP web application developers. This is a big step for SAP to move from WebDynpro to UI5 development. All in one Fiori and UI5 technology are a big step of SAP because Fiori offers easy implementation, easy rollout to different devices and easy handling, thus saving time and money and minimizing the risk. Fiori also increases productivity by empowering managers and employees to get the job done anytime and anywhere. In my opinion, the development of Fiori apps will remain stable in the coming years and gain a great importance in the wide market.

6   Future prospect

For the future research, it would be interesting to find out how different is the development between SAP Fiori apps and WebDynpro and which great advantages were not taken into Fiori apps. We have found out, that Transactional Fiori apps can run on any database who support SAP ERP. It would be interesting to find out where the big differences between SAP HANA and other databases are. The relationship between SAP GUI and Fiori apps is not one-to-one. In this seminar, we found, that in one SAP GUI transaction may be multiple Fiori apps include, or multiple SAP GUI transaction into a single Fiori app. So, it would good to list some Fiori app with this situation to see the differences.

7   Sources

7.1   Print sources

[1] Jeske, T., (2005) SAP für Java-Entwickler: Konzepte, Schnittstellen, Technologien, Verlag Springer, pp. 7.

[2] Zairi M., et. al., (2000) The effective application of SAP R/3: a proposed model of best practice, Vol. 13 Number 3 pp. 156-167.

[3] Mathew, B. (2015) Beginning SAP Fiori, Apress, pp. 12-13.

[4] Gellert, U. (2013) Web Dynpro Abap for Practitioners, Springer-Verlag Berlin and Heidelberg GmbH & Co. K, p. 4.

7.2   Online sources

[5] SAP SE, (2009-2016) SAPUI5 vs. OpenUI5 (retrieved on 28th November 2016)

https://openui5.hana.ondemand.com/#docs/guide/5982a9734748474aa8d4af9c3d8f31c0.html

[6] Elango, S. (n. d.) SAPUI5 Community – Featured Content (retrieved on 12th December 2016) http://www.sap.com/community/topic/ui5.html

[7] Behrndt, J. (2015) Was ist SAP Fiori? (retrieved on 13th December 2016)

http://mission-mobile.de/sap-fiori/#

[8] Moy, J. (2016) Keeping the faith with Fiori (retrieved on 13th December 2016)

http://www.bluet.com.au/2016/12/05/keeping-the-faith-with-fiori/

[9] SAP SE, (2013) SAP Fiori Simplifies the Enterprise Software Experience With Customer-Sytle Apps ((retrieved on 15th January 2017)

https://news.sap.com/sap-fiori-simplifies-the-enterprise-software-experience-with-consumer-style-apps/

[10] anonym (n. d.) An Introduction to SAP (retrieved on 15th January 2017)

http://www.erpgreat.com/sap-introduction.htm

[11] Gupta, A. (2016) Overview of SAP Fiori Design Elements (retrieved on 11th January 2017)

   http://smartphonebizapps.com/sap-fiori-development/overview-of-sap-fiori-design-elements

[12] SAP SE, (2016) Fiori Design Guidelines (retrieved on 17th January 2017)

   https://experience.sap.com/fiori-design/

[13] Liebscher, R., (2016) SAP Fiori – App für das ERP (retrieved on 18th January 2017)

   https://www.sogehtsoftware.de/blog/post/sap-fiori-apps-fuer-das-erp

[14] Behrndt, J. (n. d.) SAP Fiori: HCM Apps für die neue Generation (retrieved on 17th January 2017)

   http://mission-mobile.de/files/downloads/2015/06/SAP_Fiori_HCM_Apps_mindsquare.pdf

YOUR KNOWLEDGE HAS VALUE

Today almost every software and websites has a mobile compatible version and everyone can check anything on his mobile or tablet. This wasn't the case 7-8 years ago. For SAP, Graphical User Interface as known as GUI was very powerful at the time when SAP launched its ERP software. With time, many other software exists with the fleet of HTML5 based powerful and more appealing modern UI-technology. For this, the old GUI was not able to stand with it. (...)

www.grin.com

Document Nr. V426830
https://www.grin.com
ISBN 9783668714540

9 783668 714540